psalms
to live by

Paraphrase by
KENNETH N. TAYLOR

Compiled and arranged by
JOHN CALVIN REID

G/L REGAL REFLECTIONS

A Division of G/L Publications
Glendale, California, U.S.A.

Published by
Regal Books Division, G/L Publications
Glendale, California 91209, U.S.A.

Library of Congress Catalog Card No. 72-86211
ISBN 0-8307-0189-3

Scripture is from
The Living Bible, Paraphrased (Wheaton:
Tyndale House, Publishers, 1971). Used
by permission.

Introduction

The oldest, best known and most widely used "Prayer Book" in the world—that is the book of Psalms.

In its pages God is revealed as the ever-present and all-sufficient answer to the deepest longings and highest aspirations of the soul. Thus, down through the centuries the Psalms have proven to be both universal and timeless in their appeal to the heart.

The following selections have been chosen and captioned with the purpose of making them practical and profitable for use in personal meditation and family devotions.

It is my hope and prayer that you will find them a never-failing source of strength and inspiration as you climb the altar stairs that lead to God.

John Calvin Reid

Contents

God's Perfect Laws   6
Evening Meditation   9
Morning Meditation   10
Message from Outer Space   11
Before Worship   13
Prayer for a Friend   15
God My Shepherd   16
Friendship with God   18
Thanksgiving for
  Health Restored   20
Honest Confession   22
God Answers Prayer   24
The Fountain of Life   26
Don't Worry!   27
How Great God Is!   29
Don't Be Discouraged   31

What God Wants 33
For Forgiveness
  and Cleansing 34
Until the Storm Is Past 36
God My Rock 39
Longing for God 41
Harvest Song 42
Sunset Years 45
When the Wicked Prosper 17
In Your Temple 49
Prayer for Revival 51
Prayer for Recovery 52
Shielded by His Wings 54
Thanksgiving Morning
  and Evening 56
Come, Let Us Worship 57
A Noble Resolve 59
Bless the Lord! 60
The Lord of Creation 63
Pathway to Happiness 65
Day and Night Guardian 67
When God's People Worship 68
Within the Family Circle 71
The All-Knowing and
  the All-Loving 73
Depressed but Hopeful 75
Gloria in Excelsis 77
Hallelujah Chorus 79

God's Perfect Laws

Oh, the joys of those who do not follow evil men's advice, who do not hang around with sinners, scoffing at the things of God. But they delight in doing everything God wants them to and day and night are always meditating on His laws and thinking about ways to follow Him more closely. They are like trees along a river bank bearing luscious fruit each season without fail. Their leaves shall never wither, and all they do shall prosper.

God's laws are perfect. They protect us, make us wise and give us joy and light. God's laws are just and perfect. Reverence for God keeps us pure and

leads us on to heaven. His laws are more desirable than gold. They are sweeter than honey dripping from a honeycomb. For they warn us away from harm and give success to those who obey them!

But how can I ever know what sins are lurking in my heart? Cleanse me from these hidden faults. And keep me from deliberate wrongs; help me to stop doing them. Only then can I be free of guilt and innocent of some great crime. May my spoken words and unspoken thoughts be pleasing even to You, O Lord, my Rock and my Redeemer.

From Psalms, 1, 19

Evening Meditation

O God, You have always cared for me in my distress; now hear me as I call again. Have mercy on me. Hear my prayer. So many say that God will never help me. But Lord, You are my shield, my glory and my only hope. I will lie down in peace and sleep, for though I am alone, O Lord, You will keep me safely. For salvation comes from God. What joys He gives to all His people!

From Psalms 4, 3

Morning Meditation

O Lord, hear me praying; listen to
my plea, O God my King, for I will
never pray to anyone but You. Each
morning I will look to You in heaven
and lay my requests before You,
praying earnestly. Lord, lead me as
You promised me You would. Tell me
clearly what to do, which way to turn.
Make everyone rejoice who puts his
trust in You. Fill all who love You
with Your happiness.

From Psalm 5

Message from Outer Space

The heavens are telling the glory of God; they are a marvelous display of His craftsmanship. Day and night they keep on telling about God. Without a sound or word, silent in the skies, their message reaches out to all the world. The sun lives in the heavens where God placed it and moves out across the skies as radiant as a bridegroom going to his wedding, or as joyous as an athlete looking forward to a race! The sun crosses the heavens from end to end, and nothing can hide from its heat.

O Lord our God, the majesty and glory of Your name fills all the earth and overflows the heavens. You have taught the little children to praise You perfectly. May their example shame and silence Your enemies! When I look up into the night skies and see the work of Your fingers—the moon and the stars You have made—I cannot understand how You can bother with mere puny man, to pay any attention to him!

And yet You have made him only a little lower than the angels and placed a crown of glory and honor upon his head. You have put him in charge of everything You made; everything is put under his authority:

> All sheep and oxen and wild animals, too,
>
> The birds and fish and all the life in the sea.

O Jehovah, our Lord, the majesty and glory of Your name fills the earth.

From Psalms 19, 8

Before Worship

Lord, who may go and find refuge
and shelter in Your tabernacle up on
Your holy hill? Anyone who leads a
blameless life and is truly sincere.
Anyone who refuses to slander others,
does not listen to gossip, never harms
his neighbor; speaks out against sin,
criticizes those committing it,
commends the faithful followers of the
Lord, keeps a promise even if it ruins
him; does not crush his debtors with
high interest rates, and refuses to
testify against the innocent despite the
bribes offered him—such a man shall
stand firm forever.

The earth belongs to God! Everything in all the world is His! He is the One who pushed the oceans back to let dry land appear. Who may climb the mountain of the Lord and enter where He lives? Who may stand before the Lord? Only those with pure hands and hearts, who do not practice dishonesty and lying. They will receive God's own goodness as their blessing from Him, planted in their lives by God Himself, their Saviour.

Open up, O ancient gates, and let the King of Glory in. Who is this King of Glory? The Lord, strong and mighty, invincible in battle. Yes, open wide the gates and let the King of Glory in. Who is this King of Glory? The Commander of all of heaven's armies!

From Psalms 15, 24

Prayer for a Friend

In your day of trouble, may the Lord be with you! May God keep you from all harm. May He send you aid from His sanctuary in Zion. May He remember with pleasure the gifts you have given Him, your sacrifices and burnt offerings. May He grant you your heart's desire and fulfill all your plans. May there be shouts of joy when we hear the news of your victory, flags flying with praise to God for all that He has done for you. May He answer all your prayers!

From Psalm 20

15

God My Shepherd

Because the Lord is my shepherd, I have everything I need! He lets me rest in the meadow grass and leads me beside the quiet streams. He restores my failing health. He helps me do what honors Him the most. Even when walking through the dark valley of death I will not be afraid, for You are close beside me, guarding, guiding all the way. You provide delicious food for me in the presence of my enemies. You have welcomed me as Your guest; blessings overflow! Your goodness and unfailing kindness shall be with me all of my life, and afterwards I will live with You forever in Your home.

From Psalm 23

Friendship with God

To You, O Lord, I pray! Don't fail me, Lord, for I am trusting You. Show me the path where I should go, O Lord; point out the right road for me to walk. Lead me; teach me; for You are the God who gives me salvation. I have no hope except in You. Overlook my youthful sins, O Lord! Look at me instead through eyes of mercy and forgiveness, through eyes of everlasting love and kindness.

The Lord is good and glad to teach the proper path to all who go astray; He will teach the ways that are right and best to those who humbly turn to

Him. And when we obey Him, every path He guides us on is fragrant with His loving-kindness and His truth.

But Lord, my sins! How many they are. Oh, pardon them for the honor of Your name. Where is the man who fears the Lord? God will teach him how to choose the best! He shall live within God's circle of blessing, and his children shall inherit the earth! Friendship with God is reserved for those who reverence Him. With them alone He shares the secrets of His promises.

My eyes are ever looking to the Lord for help, for He alone can rescue me. Come, Lord, and show me Your mercy, for I am helpless, overwhelmed, in deep distress; my problems go from bad to worse. Oh, save me from them all! See my sorrows; feel my pain; forgive my sins. Assign me godliness and integrity as my bodyguards, for I expect You to protect me. Oh, let it never be said that I trusted You in vain!

From Psalm 25

Thanksgiving
for Health Restored

O Lord my God, I pled with You, and You gave me my health again. You brought me back from the brink of the grave, from death itself, and here I am alive! Oh, sing to Him you saints of His; give thanks to His holy name. His anger lasts a moment; His favor lasts for life! Weeping may go on all night, but in the morning there is joy.

In my prosperity I said, "This is forever; nothing can stop me now! The Lord has shown me His favor. He has made me steady as a mountain."

Then, Lord, You turned Your face
away from me and cut off Your river
of blessings. Suddenly my courage was
gone; I was terrified and panic-
stricken. I cried to You, O Lord;
oh, how I pled, "Hear me, Lord; oh,
have pity and help me." Then He
turned my sorrow into joy! He took
away my clothes of mourning and
gave me gay and festive garments to
rejoice in so that I might sing glad
praises to the Lord instead of lying in
silence in the grave. O Lord my God,
I will keep on thanking You forever!

Blessed is the Lord, for He has
shown me that His never-failing love
protects me like the walls of a fort! I
spoke too hastily when I said, "The
Lord has deserted me," for You
listened to my plea and answered me.
Oh, love the Lord all of you who are
His people; for the Lord protects those
who are loyal to Him, but harshly
punishes all who haughtily reject Him.
So cheer up! Take courage if you are
depending on the Lord!

From Psalms 30, 31

Honest Confession

What happiness for those whose guilt has been forgiven! What joys when sins are covered over! What relief for those who have confessed their sins and God has cleared their record. There was a time when I wouldn't admit what a sinner I was. But my dishonesty made me miserable and filled my days with frustration. All day and all night Your hand was heavy on me. My strength evaporated like water on a sunny day until I finally admitted all my sins to You and stopped trying to hide them. I said to myself, "I will confess them to the Lord." And You forgave me! All my guilt is gone!

After this experience, I say that every believer should confess his sins to God as soon as he becomes aware of them, while there is yet time to be forgiven. If he does this, judgment will not touch him. You are my hiding place from every storm of life; You even keep me from getting into trouble! You surround me with songs of victory. Abiding love surrounds those who trust the Lord. So rejoice in Him, all those who are His, and shout for joy, all those who try to obey Him.

From Psalm 32

God Answers Prayer

I will praise the Lord no matter
what happens. I will constantly speak
of His glories and grace. I will boast of
all His kindness to me. Let all who are
discouraged take heart! Let us praise
the Lord together and exalt His name.
For I cried to Him and He answered
me! He freed me from all my fears.
Others too were radiant at what He
did for them. Theirs was no downcast
look of rejection! This poor man cried
to the Lord—and the Lord heard him
and saved him out of his troubles. For

the Angel of the Lord guards and rescues all who reverence Him.

Sons and daughters, come and listen and let me teach you the importance of trusting and fearing the Lord. Do you want a long, good life? Then watch your tongue! Keep your lips from lying. Turn from all known sin and spend your time in doing good. Try to live in peace with everyone; work hard at it. For the eyes of the Lord are intently watching all who live good lives, and He gives attention when they cry to Him.

Yes, the Lord hears the good man when he calls to Him for help and saves him out of all his troubles. The Lord is close to those whose hearts are breaking; He rescues those who are humbly sorry for their sins. The good man does not escape all troubles—he has them too. But the Lord helps him in each and every one. As for those who serve the Lord, He will redeem them; everyone who takes refuge in Him will be freely pardoned.

From Psalm 34

The Fountain of Life

Your steadfast love, O Lord, is as
great as all the heavens. Your
faithfulness reaches beyond the clouds!
Your justice is as solid as God's
mountains. Your decisions are as full
of wisdom as the oceans are with
water. You are the Fountain of Life;
our light is from Your Light. Pour out
Your unfailing love on those who
know You! Never stop giving Your
salvation to those who long to do
Your will.

From Psalm 36

Don't Worry!

Never envy the wicked! Soon they
fade away like grass and disappear.
Trust in the Lord instead. Be kind and
good to others; then you will live
safely here in the land and prosper,
feeding in safety. Be delighted with
the Lord! Then He will give you all
your heart's desires. Commit
everything you do to the Lord. Trust
Him to help you do it and He will.
Your innocence will be clear to
everyone. He will vindicate you with
the blazing light of justice shining
down as from the noonday sun. Rest

in the Lord; wait patiently for Him to act. Don't be envious of evil men who prosper. Stop your anger! Turn off your wrath. Don't fret and worry—it only leads to harm.

Don't be impatient for the Lord to act! Keep steadily along His pathway and in due season He will honor you with every blessing, and you will see the wicked destroyed. I myself have seen it happen; a proud and evil man towering like a cedar of Lebanon, but when I looked again, he was gone! I searched but could not find him! But the good man—what a different story! For the good man—the blameless, the upright, the man of peace—he has a wonderful future ahead of him. For him there is a happy ending. The Lord saves the godly! He is their salvation and their refuge when trouble comes. Because they trust in Him, He helps them and delivers them from the plots of evil men.

From Psalm 37

How Great God Is!

I waited patiently for God to help me; then He listened and heard my cry. He lifted me out of the pit of despair, out from the bog and the mire and set my feet on a hard, firm path and steadied me as I walked along. He has given me a new song to sing, of praises to our God. Now many will hear of the glorious things He did for me. O Lord my God, many and many a time You have done great miracles for us, and we are ever in Your thoughts. Who else can do such glorious things? No one else can be compared with You. There isn't time to tell of all Your wonderful deeds.

It isn't sacrifices and offerings which You really want from Your people. Burnt animals bring no special joy to Your heart. But You have accepted the offer of my lifelong service. Then I said, "See, I have come, just as all the prophets foretold. And I delight to do Your will, my God; for Your law is written upon My heart!" I have told everyone the good news that You forgive men's sins. I have not been timid about it, as You well know, O Lord. I have not kept this good news hidden in my heart, but have proclaimed Your loving-kindness and truth to all the congregation.

O Lord, don't hold back Your tender mercies from me! My only hope is in Your love and faithfulness! May the joy of the Lord be given to everyone who loves Him and His salvation. May they constantly exclaim, "How great God is!"

From Psalm 40

Don't Be Discouraged

As the deer pants for water, so I long for You, O God. I thirst for God, the living God. Where can I find Him to come and stand before Him? Day and night I weep for His help, while my enemies taunt me. "Where is this God of yours?" they scoff. Take courage, my soul! Do you remember those times (but how could you ever forget them!) when you led a great procession to the Temple on festival days, singing with joy, praising the Lord? Why then be downcast? Why be discouraged and sad? Hope in God! I shall yet praise Him again? Yes, I shall again praise Him for His help.

O my soul, don't be discouraged!
Don't be upset! Expect God to act!
For I know that I shall again have
plenty of reason to praise Him for all
that He will do! He is my help! He is
my God! Oh, send out Your light and
Your truth—let them lead me. Let
them lead me to Your Temple on Your
holy mountain, Zion. There I will go
to the altar of God my exceeding joy,
and praise Him with my harp. O
God—my God! O my soul, why be so
gloomy and discouraged? Trust in
God! I shall again praise Him for His
wondrous help; He will make me
smile again, for He is my God!

From Psalms 42, 43

What God Wants

O My people, listen! For I am
your God. Listen! I have no complaint
about the sacrifices you bring to My
altar, for you bring them regularly.
But I don't need your sacrifices of
flesh and blood! What I want from
you is your true thanks; I want your
promises fulfilled. I want you to trust
Me in your times of trouble so I can
rescue you, and you can give Me
glory! True praise is a worthy
sacrifice; this really honors Me. Those
who walk in My paths will receive
salvation from the Lord.

From Psalm 50

For Forgiveness and Cleansing

O loving and kind God, have mercy. Have pity upon me and take away the awful stain of my transgressions. Oh, wash me, cleanse me from this guilt. Let me be pure again. For I admit my shameful deed—it haunts me day and night. It is against You and You alone I sinned and did this terrible thing. You saw it all, and Your sentence against me is just. But I was born a sinner, yes, from the moment my mother conceived me. You deserve honesty from the heart; yes, utter sincerity and truthfulness. Oh, give me this wisdom.

Sprinkle me with the cleansing blood and I shall be clean again. Wash me and I shall be whiter than snow. And after You have punished me, give me back my joy again. Don't keep looking at my sins—erase them from Your sight.

Create in me a new, clean heart, O God, filled with clean thoughts and right desires. Don't toss me aside, banished forever from Your presence. Don't take Your Holy Spirit from me. Restore to me again the joy of Your salvation, and make me willing to obey You. Then I will teach Your ways to other sinners, and they—guilty like me—will repent and return to You.

Don't sentence me to death, O my God, You alone can rescue me. Then I will sing of Your forgiveness, for my lips will be unsealed—oh, how I will praise You. You don't want penance. If You did, how gladly I would do it! You aren't interested in offerings burned before You on the altar. It is a broken spirit You want—remorse and penitence. A broken and a contrite heart, O God, You will not ignore.

From Psalm 51

Until the Storm Is Past

O God, have pity, for I am trusting You! I will hide beneath the shadow of Your wings until this storm is past. I will cry to the God of heaven who does such wonders for me. He will send down help from heaven to save me because of His love and His faithfulness. O God, my heart is quiet and confident. No wonder I can sing Your praises! Rouse yourself, my soul! Arise, O harp and lyre! Let us greet the dawn with song! I will thank You publicly throughout the land. I will sing Your praises among the nations. Your kindness and love are as vast as

the heavens. Your faithfulness is higher than the skies. Yes, be exalted, O God, above the heavens. May Your glory shine throughout the earth.

I will surely do what I have promised, Lord, and thank You for Your help. You have seen me tossing and turning through the night. You have collected all my tears and preserved them in Your bottle! You have recorded every one in Your book. You have saved me from death and my feet from slipping so that I can walk before the Lord in the land of the living. Blessed be God who didn't turn away when I was praying and didn't refuse me His kindness and love.

From Psalms 57, 56

God My Rock

I stand silently before the Lord,
waiting for Him to rescue me. For
salvation comes from Him alone. Yes,
He alone is my rock, my rescuer,
defense and fortress. Why then should
I be tense with fear when troubles
come?

O God, listen to me! Hear my
prayer! For wherever I am, though far
away at the ends of the earth, I will
cry to You for help. When my heart is
faint and overwhelmed, lead me to the
mighty, towering rock of safety. For
You are my refuge, a high tower
where my enemies can never reach
me. I shall live forever in Your
tabernacle; oh, to be safe beneath the

shelter of Your wings! For You have heard my vows, O God, to praise You every day, and You have given me the blessings You reserve for those who reverence Your name. You will give me added years of life as rich and full as those of many generations all packed into one! And I shall live before the Lord forever. Oh, send Your loving-kindness and truth to guard and watch over me, and I will praise Your name continually, fulfilling my vow of praising You each day.

Blessed be God who didn't turn away when I was praying and didn't refuse me His kindness and love. Yes, He alone is my rock, my rescuer, defense and fortress—when then should I be tense with fear when troubles come? My protection and success come from God alone. He is my refuge, a rock where no enemy can reach me. Give your burdens to the Lord. He will carry them. He will not permit the godly to slip or fall.

From Psalms 62, 61, 66, 55

Longing for God

O God, *my* God! How I long to find You! For Your love and kindness are better to me than life itself. I will bless You as long as I live, lifting up my hands to You in prayer. At last I shall be fully satisfied; I will praise You with great joy! I lie awake at night thinking of You—Oh, how much you have helped me—and how I rejoice through the night beneath the protecting shadow of Your wings!

From Psalm 63

Harvest Song

Sing to the Lord, all the earth!
Sing of His glorious name! Tell the
world how wonderful He is. How
awe-inspiring are Your deeds, O God!
How great Your power! All the earth
shall worship You and sing of Your
glories. Come, see the glorious things
God has done. What marvelous
miracles happen to His people!

He formed the mountains by His
mighty strength. He quiets the raging
oceans and all the world's clamor. In
the farthest corners of the earth the
glorious acts of God shall startle
everyone. The dawn and sunset shout

for joy! He waters the earth to make it fertile. The rivers of God will not run dry! He prepares the earth for His people and sends them rich harvests of grain. He waters the furrows with abundant rain. Showers soften the earth, melting the clods and causing seeds to sprout across the land. Then He crowns it all with green, lush pastures in the wilderness; hillsides blossom with joy. The pastures are filled with flocks of sheep, and the valleys are carpeted with grain.

Praise God, O world! May all the peoples of the earth give thanks to You. For the earth has yielded abundant harvests. God, even our own God, will bless us. And peoples from remotest lands will worship Him.

From Psalms 66, 65, 67

Sunset Years

Lord, You are my refuge! Don't let me down! Rescue me! Bend down Your ear and listen to my plea and save me. Be to me a great protecting rock, where I am always welcome. O Lord, You alone are my hope; I've trusted You from childhood.

All day long I'll praise and honor You, O God, for all that You have done for me. And now, in my old age, don't set me aside! Don't forsake me now when my strength is failing! Don't let the floods overwhelm me or the ocean swallow me; save me from the pit that threatens me. O Jehovah, answer my prayers, for Your loving-kindness is wonderful; Your mercy is so plentiful, so tender and so kind.

O God, You have helped me from my earliest childhood—and I have constantly testified to others of the wonderful things You do. And now that I am old and gray, don't forsake me. Give me time to tell this new generation (and their children too) about all Your mighty miracles. Your power and goodness, Lord, reach to the highest heavens. You have done such wonderful things. Where is there another God like You?

You have let me sink down deep in desperate problems. But You will bring me back to live again, up from the depths of the earth. You will give me greater honor than before. And You will turn again and comfort me. I will praise You with music, telling of Your faithfulness to all Your promises. I will talk to others all day long about Your justice and Your goodness. The Lord will work out His plans for my life—for Your loving-kindness, Lord, continues forever. Don't abandon me—for You made me.

From Psalms 71, 69, 138

When the Wicked Prosper

How good God is to Israel—to those whose hearts are pure. But as for me, my feet were slipping and I was almost gone. For I was envious of the prosperity of the proud and wicked. Yes, all through life their road is smooth! They grow sleek and fat. Their pride sparkles like a jeweled necklace, and their clothing is woven of cruelty! These fat cats have everything their hearts could ever wish for! They scoff at God and threaten His people. How proudly they speak! They boast against the very heavens, and their words strut through the earth. And so God's people are dismayed and confused and drink it all in.

It is so hard to explain it—this prosperity of those who hate the Lord. Then one day I went into God's sanctuary to meditate and thought about the future of these evil men. What a slippery path they are on—suddenly God will send them sliding over the edge of the cliff and down to their destruction: an instant end to all their happiness, an eternity of terror.

You are holding my right hand! You will keep on guiding me all my life with Your wisdom and counsel; and afterwards receive me into the glories of heaven! Whom have I in heaven but You? And I desire no one on earth as much as You! My health fails; my spirit droops, yet God remains! He is the strength of my heart; He is mine forever! I get as close to Him as I can! I have chosen Him and I will tell everyone about the wonderful ways He rescues me.

From Psalm 73

In Your Temple

How lovely is Your Temple, O
Lord of the armies of heaven. I long,
yes, faint with longing to be able to
enter Your courtyard and come near
to the Living God. Even the sparrows
and swallows are welcome to come
and nest among Your altars and there
have their young, O Lord of heaven's
armies, my King and my God! How
happy are Your priests who can
always be in Your Temple, singing
Your praises! Happy are those who
are strong in the Lord, who want
above all else to follow Your steps.

When they walk through the Valley of Weeping it will become a place of springs where pools of blessing and refreshment collect after rains! They will grow constantly in strength and each of them is invited to meet with the Lord in Zion! O Jehovah, God of the heavenly armies, hear my prayer! Listen, God of Israel. O God, our defender and our shield, have mercy.

A single day spent in Your Temple is better than a thousand anywhere else! I would rather be a doorman of the Temple of my God than live in palaces of wickedness. For Jehovah God is our light and our protector. He gives us grace and glory. No good thing will He withhold from those who walk along His paths. O Lord of the armies of heaven, blessed are those who trust in You.

Hallelujah! Yes, let His people praise Him, as they stand in His Temple courts. Praise the Lord because He is so good; sing to His wonderful name.

From Psalms 84, 135

Prayer for Revival

Lord, You have poured out amazing blessings on this land! You have forgiven the sins of Your people—yes, covered over each one. Now bring us back to loving You, O Lord, so that Your anger never need rise against us again. Surely Your salvation is near to those who reverence You; our land will be filled with Your glory! Oh, revive us! Then Your people can rejoice in You again. Pour out Your love and kindness on us, Lord, and grant us Your salvation.

From Psalm 85

Prayer for Recovery

Lord, hear my prayer! Listen to my plea! Don't turn away from me in this time of my distress. Bend down Your ear and give me speedy answers, for my days disappear like smoke. My health is broken and my heart is sick; it is trampled like grass and is withered. My food is tasteless, and I have lost my appetite. I am reduced to skin and bones because of all my groaning and despair. I am like a vulture in a far-off wilderness or like an owl alone in the desert. I lie awake, lonely as a solitary sparrow on the roof.

My eyes grow dim with weeping. Each day I beg Your help; O Lord, I reach my pleading hands to You for mercy. Soon it will be too late! Of what use are Your miracles when I am in the grave? How can I praise You then? Can those in the grave declare Your loving-kindness? Can they proclaim Your faithfulness? Can the darkness speak of Your miracles? Can anyone in the Land of Forgetfulness talk about Your help? O Lord, I plead for my life and shall keep on pleading day by day.

Hear my prayer, O Lord; listen to my cry! Don't sit back, unmindful of my tears! For I am Your guest! I am a traveler passing through the earth as all my fathers were! Spare me, Lord! Let me recover and be filled with happiness again. I am poor and needy, yet the Lord is thinking about me right now! O my God, You are my helper! You are my Saviour; come quickly and save me. Please don't delay!

From Psalms 88, 102, 40

Shielded by His Wings

We live within the shadow of the
Almighty, sheltered by the God who is
above all gods. This I declare, that He
alone is my refuge, my place of safety;
He is my God, and I am trusting Him.
For He rescues you from every trap
and protects you from the fatal plague.
He will shield you with His wings!
They will shelter you. His faithful
promises are your armor.

Now you don't need to be afraid of
the dark any more, nor fear the
dangers of the day; nor dread the
plagues of darkness, nor disasters in
the morning, for He orders His angels
to protect you wherever you go. They
will steady you with their hands to
keep you from stumbling against the

rocks on the trail. You can safely meet a lion or step on poisonous snakes; yes, even trample them beneath your feet!

For the Lord says, "Because he loves Me, I will rescue him; I will make him great because he trusts in My name. When he calls on Me I will answer; I will be with him in trouble, rescue him and honor him. I will satisfy him with a full life and give him My salvation."

Jehovah is my refuge! I choose the God above all gods to shelter me.

From Psalm 91

Thanksgiving Morning and Evening

It is good to say, "Thank You" to the Lord, to sing praises to the God who is above all gods. Every morning tell Him, "Thank You for Your kindness," and every evening rejoice in all His faithfulness. Sing His praises, accompanied by music from the harp and lute and lyre. You have done so much for me, O Lord. No wonder I am glad! I sing for joy. O Lord, what miracles You do! And how deep are Your thoughts! The Lord continues forever, exalted in the heavens.

From Psalm 92

Come, Let Us Worship

Oh, come, let us sing to the Lord! Give a joyous shout in honor of the rock of our salvation! Come before Him with thankful hearts. Let us sing Him psalms of praise. For the Lord is a great God, the great King of all gods. He controls the formation of the depths of the earth and the mightiest mountains; all are His. He made the sea and formed the land; they too are His. Come, kneel before the Lord our Maker, for He is our God. We are His sheep and He is our shepherd! Oh, that you would hear Him calling you today and come to Him! For the Lord

is great and greatly to be praised.
Worship only Him. Worship the Lord
with the beauty of holy lives. Let the
earth tremble before Him.

Shout with joy before the Lord, O
earth! Obey Him gladly; come before
Him singing with joy. Try to realize
what this means—the Lord is God! He
made us—we are His people, the sheep
of His pasture. Go through His open
gates with great thanksgiving; enter
His courts with praise. Give thanks to
Him and bless His name. For the Lord
is always good. He is always loving
and kind, and His faithfulness goes on
and on to each succeeding generation.

From Psalms 95, 96, 97, 100

A Noble Resolve

I will sing Your praises! I will try to walk a blameless path, but how I need Your help—especially in my own home where I long to act as I should. Help me to refuse the low and vulgar things; help me to abhor all crooked deals of every kind, to have no part in them. I will reject all selfishness and stay away from every evil. I will make the godly of the land my heroes and invite them to my home. Those who are truly good shall be my examples.

From Psalm 101

Bless the Lord!

I bless the holy name of God with all my heart. Yes, I will bless the Lord and not forget the glorious things He does for me. He forgives all my sins! He heals me! He ransoms me from hell! He surrounds me with loving-kindness and tender mercies!
He fills my life with good things! My youth is renewed like the eagle's! He gives justice to all who are treated unfairly.

He revealed His will and nature to Moses and the people of Israel. He is merciful and tender toward those who don't deserve it; He is slow to get angry and full of kindness and love! He never bears a grudge, nor remains angry forever. He has not punished us

as we deserve for all our sins, for His mercy towards those who fear and honor Him is as great as the height of the heavens above the earth. He has removed our sins as far away from us as the east is from the west. He is like a father to us, tender and sympathetic to those who reverence Him.

For He knows we are but dust, and that our days are few and brief, like grass, like flowers, blown by the wind and gone forever. But the loving-kindness of the Lord is from everlasting to everlasting to those who reverence Him; His salvation is to children's children of those who are faithful to His covenant and remember to obey Him!

The Lord has made the heavens His throne; from there He rules over everything there is. Bless the Lord, you mighty angels of His who carry out His orders, listening for each of His commands. Let everything everywhere bless the Lord. And how I bless Him, too!

From Psalm 103

The Lord of Creation

I bless the Lord: O Lord my God,
how great You are! You are robed
with honor and with majesty and
light! You stretched out the starry
curtain of the heavens, and hollowed
out the surface of the earth to form
the seas. The clouds are His chariots!
He rides upon the wings of the wind!
You bound the world together so that
it would never fall apart. You clothed
the earth with floods of waters
covering up the mountains. You spoke,
and at the sound of Your shout the
water collected into its vast ocean
beds. Mountains rose and valleys sank
to the levels You decreed. And then
You set a boundary for the seas, so

that they would never again cover the earth.

There before me lies the mighty ocean, teeming with life of every kind, both great and small. And look! See the ships! And over there, the whale You made to play in the sea! Every one of these depends on You to give them daily food. You supply it, and they gather it! You open wide Your hand to feed them and they are satisfied with all Your bountiful provision.

O Lord, what a variety You have made! And in wisdom You have made them all! The earth is full of Your riches. Praise God forever! How He must rejoice in all His work! I will sing to the Lord as long as I live! I will praise God to my last breath! May He be pleased by all these thoughts about Him, for He is the source of all my joy. I will praise Him. Hallelujah!

From Psalm 104

Pathway to Happiness

Happy are all who perfectly follow the laws of God. Happy are all who search for God and always do His will, rejecting compromise with evil and walking only in His paths. You have given us Your laws to obey—Oh, how I want to follow them consistently. Then I will not be disgraced, for I will have a clean record. After You have corrected me I will thank You by living as I should! I will obey! Oh, don't forsake me and let me slip back into sin again.

How can a young man stay pure? By reading Your Word and following its rules. I have tried my best to find You—don't let me wander off from

Your instructions. I have thought much about Your words, and stored them in my heart so that they would hold me back from sin. Blessed Lord, teach me Your rules. Open my eyes to see wonderful things in Your Word. I am but a pilgrim here on earth: how I need a map—and Your commands are my chart and guide.

Lord, deal with me in loving-kindness, and teach me, Your servant, to obey; for I am Your servant, therefore give me common sense to apply Your rules to everything I do. I praise You for letting me learn Your laws. I will sing about their wonder, for each of them is just. Stand ready to help me because I have chosen to follow Your will. O Lord, I have longed for Your salvation and Your law is my delight. If You will let me live, I will praise You; let Your laws assist me. I have wandered away like a lost sheep; come and find me for I have not turned away from Your commandments.

From Psalm 119

Day and Night Guardian

Shall I look to the mountains for help? No! My help is from Jehovah who made the mountains! And the heavens too! O God, I lift my eyes to You.

He will never let you stumble, slip or fall. For He is always watching, never sleeping. Jehovah Himself is caring for you! He protects you day and night. He keeps you from all evil and preserves your life. He keeps His eye upon you as you come and go and always guards you. Our help is from the Lord who made heaven and earth!

From Psalm 121

When God's People Worship

I was glad for the suggestion of going to Jerusalem to the Temple of the Lord. Now we are standing here inside the crowded city. All Israel—Jehovah's people—have come to worship as the law requires, to thank and praise the Lord. Those who trust in the Lord are steady as Mount Zion, unmoved by any circumstance. Just as the mountains surround and protect Jerusalem, so the Lord surrounds and protects His people.

Pray for the peace of Jerusalem. May all who love this city prosper. O

Jerusalem, may there be peace within your walls and prosperity in your palaces. This I ask for the sake of all my brothers and my friends who live here; and may there be peace as a protection to the Temple of the Lord.

Oh, bless the Lord, you who serve Him as watchmen in the Temple every night. Lift your hands in holiness and bless the Lord. The Lord bless you from Zion—the Lord who made heaven and earth.

From Psalms 122, 125, 134

Within the Family Circle

Blessings on all who reverence and trust the Lord—on all who obey Him! Their reward shall be prosperity and happiness. Your wife shall be contented in your home. And look at all those children! There they sit around the dinner table as vigorous and healthy as young olive trees.

Children are a gift from God; they are His reward. Children born to a young man are like sharp arrows to defend him. Happy is the man who has his quiver full of them. That man shall have the help he needs. That is God's reward to those who reverence and trust Him. May the Lord

continually bless you with heaven's
blessings as well as with human joys.
May you live to enjoy your
grandchildren! And may God bless
Israel!

How wonderful it is, how pleasant,
when brothers live in harmony! For
harmony is as precious as the fragrant
anointing oil that was poured over
Aaron's head and ran down onto his
beard and onto the border of his robe.
Harmony is as refreshing as the dew
on Mount Hermon on the mountains
of Israel. And God has pronounced
this eternal blessing on Jerusalem,
even life forevermore.

I am quiet now before the Lord, just
as a child who is weaned from the
breast. Yes, my begging has been
stilled. You too should quietly trust in
the Lord—now, and always.

From Psalms 128, 127, 133, 131

The All-Knowing and the All-Loving

O Lord, You have examined my heart and know everything about me. When far away You know my every thought. You chart the path ahead of me, and tell me where to stop and rest! Every moment, You know where I am! You both precede and follow me and place Your hand of blessing on my head. This is too glorious, too wonderful to believe!

I can never be lost to Your Spirit! I can never get away from God! If I go up to heaven You are there; if I go down to the place of the dead, You are there. If I ride the morning winds to the farthest oceans, even there Your hand will guide me, Your strength will support me. If I try to hide in the darkness, the night becomes light around me! For even darkness cannot hide from God. Darkness and light are both alike to You.

You made all the delicate, inner parts of my body and knit them together in my mother's womb. Thank You for making me so wonderfully complex! You saw me before I was born and scheduled each day of my life before I began to breathe. Every day was recorded in Your book!

How precious it is, Lord, to realize that You are thinking about me constantly! I can't even count how many times a day Your thoughts turn towards me! And when I waken in the morning, You are still thinking of me! Search me, O God, and know my heart. Test my thoughts. Point out anything You find in me that makes You sad, and lead me along the path of everlasting life.

From Psalm 139

Depressed but Hopeful

How I plead with God, how I implore His mercy, pouring out my troubles before Him. For I am overwhelmed and desperate, and You alone know which way I ought to turn. I am losing all hope; I am paralyzed with fear. I remember the glorious miracles You did in days of long ago. I reach out for You. I thirst for You as parched land thirsts for rain. Come quickly, Lord, and answer me, for my depression deepens; don't turn away from me or I shall die.

Never forget Your promises to me, Your servant; for they are my only hope. They give me strength in all my troubles; how they refresh and revive

me! Forever, O Lord, Your Word
stands firm in heaven. Your
faithfulness extends to every
generation, like the earth You created;
it endures by your decree, for
everything serves Your plans. I would
have despaired and perished unless
Your laws had been my deepest
delight. I will never lay aside Your
laws, for You have used them to
restore my joy and health. Oh, how I
love them! I think about them all day
long.

Hear me cry, for I am very low.
Rescue me from my persecutors, for
they are too strong for me. Bring me
out of prison so that I can thank You.
The godly will rejoice with me for all
Your help. Hear my prayer, O Lord;
answer my plea, because You are
faithful to Your promises. You are
merciful and gentle, Lord, slow in
getting angry, full of constant
loving-kindness and of truth; so look
down in pity and grant strength to
Your servant and save me.

From Psalms 142, 143, 119, 86

Gloria in Excelsis

I will praise You, my God and
King, and bless Your name each day
and forever. Great is Jehovah! Greatly
praise Him! His greatness is beyond
discovery! Let each generation tell its
children what glorious things He does.
I will meditate about Your glory,
splendor, majesty and miracles. Your
awe-inspiring deeds shall be on every
tongue; I will proclaim Your greatness.

Jehovah is kind and merciful, slow
to get angry, full of love. He is good
to everyone, and His compassion is
intertwined with everything He does.
All living things shall thank You,
Lord, and Your people will bless You.

They will talk together about the glory of Your kingdom and mention examples of Your power. They will tell about Your miracles and about the majesty and glory of Your reign. For Your kingdom never ends. You rule generation after generation. The Lord lifts the fallen and those bent beneath their loads.

The eyes of all mankind look up to You for help; You give them their food as they need it. You constantly satisfy the hunger and thirst of every living thing. The Lord is fair in everything He does and full of kindness. He is close to all who call on Him sincerely. He fulfills the desires of those who reverence and trust Him; He hears their cries for help and rescues them. He protects all those who love Him. I shall praise the Lord and call on all men everywhere to bless His holy name forever and forever.

From Psalm 145

Hallelujah Chorus

Hallelujah! Yes, praise the Lord!
Sing Him a new song. Sing His
praises, all His people. Praise the
Lord, O heavens! Praise Him from the
skies! Praise Him, all His angels, all
the armies of heaven. Praise Him, sun
and moon and all you twinkling stars.
Praise Him, skies above. Praise Him,
vapors high above the clouds. Let
everything He has made give praise to
Him! For He issued His command and
they came into being; He established
them forever and forever. His orders
will never be revoked.

And praise Him down there on
earth, you creatures of the ocean

depths. Let fire and hail, snow, rain, wind and weather, all obey. Let the mountains and hills, the fruit trees and cedars, the wild animals and cattle, the snakes and birds, the kings and all the people with their rulers and their judges, young men and maidens, old men and children—all praise the Lord together. For He alone is worthy. His glory is far greater than all of earth and heaven.

Hallelujah! Yes, praise the Lord! Praise Him in His Temple and in the heavens He made with mighty power. Praise Him for His mighty works. Praise His unequalled greatness. Praise Him with the trumpet and with lute and harp. Praise Him with the timbrels and processional. Praise Him with stringed instruments and horns. Praise Him with the cymbals, yes, loud clanging cymbals. Let everything alive give praises to the Lord! You praise Him! Hallelujah!

From Psalms 149, 148, 150